Sentence models for non-fiction writing

A practical resource for teaching writing

Christopher Youles

Although every effort has been made to ensure that website addresses are correct at time of going to press, Hachette Learning cannot be held responsible for the content of any website mentioned in this book. It is sometimes possible to find a relocated web page by typing in the address of the home page for a website in the URL window of your browser.

Hachette UK's policy is to use papers that are natural, renewable and recyclable products and made from wood grown in well-managed forests and other controlled sources. The logging and manufacturing processes are expected to conform to the environmental regulations of the country of origin.

To order, please visit www.HachetteLearning.com or contact Customer Service at education@hachette.co.uk / +44 (0)1235 827827.

ISBN: 978 1 0360 0647 1

© Christopher Youles 2025

First published in 2025 by Hachette Learning,
An Hachette UK Company
Carmelite House
50 Victoria Embankment
London EC4Y 0DZ
www.HachetteLearning.com

The authorised representative in the EEA is Hachette Ireland, 8 Castlecourt Centre, Dublin 15, D15 XTP3, Ireland (email: info@hbgi.ie)

Impression number   10 9 8 7 6 5 4 3 2 1
Year   2029 2028 2027 2026 2025

All rights reserved. Apart from any use permitted under UK copyright law, no part of this publication may be reproduced or transmitted in any form or by any means, electronic or mechanical, including photocopying and recording, or held within any information storage and retrieval system, without permission in writing from the publisher or under licence from the Copyright Licensing Agency Limited. Further details of such licences (for reprographic reproduction) may be obtained from the Copyright Licensing Agency Limited, www.cla.co.uk

Illustrations by DC Graphic Design Limited, Hextable, Kent.
Typeset in the UK.
Printed in the UK.
A catalogue record for this title is available from the British Library.

Together we unlock every learner's unique potential

At Hachette Learning (formerly Hodder Education), there's one thing we're certain about. No two students learn the same way. That's why our approach to teaching begins by recognising the needs of individuals first.

Our mission is to allow every learner to fulfil their unique potential by empowering those who teach them. From our expert teaching and learning resources to our digital educational tools that make learning easier and more accessible for all, we provide solutions designed to maximise the impact of learning for every teacher, parent and student.

Aligned to our parent company, Hachette Livre, founded in 1826, we pride ourselves on being a learning solutions provider with a global footprint.

www.hachettelearning.com

Chris Youles is a classroom teacher with 18 years of experience. He has been an assistant head, an English lead, a writing moderator, and a specialist leader in education who has worked with schools on improving their writing standards. Chris is also an experienced provider of professional development and workshops. In the past, he has written for Radio 4 and now spends his time starting but never finishing writing the great novel. Chris currently lives and works in Taiwan and divides his time evenly between blogging about writing and failing to go to the gym.

Contents

1 Introduction – how to use this book 1

2 Why do we write? 3

3 Content is king – what shall we write about? 6

4 Finding the right words – audience and purpose 12

5 Clarity – making your thinking clear 17

6 The 'problem' with English 20

7 Writing to inform – explaining it properly 24

8 Sentence models to inform 28

9 Let it flow – cohesion 44

10 The four sentence types – composition 50

11 Writing to persuade – the flowers of rhetoric 52

12 Why the writing isn't working and what to do about it 60

13 Model texts – putting it all together 67

14 Appendices 75

Sentence Models for Non-fiction Writing

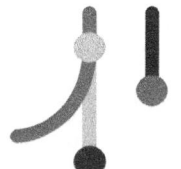 

Chapter 1
Introduction – how to use this book

Welcome to *Sentence Models for Non-fiction Writing*, your essential guide to crafting clear, concise and engaging sentences for non-fiction writing.

Here are some ideas for how to use this book:

- Explore the theory – review the writing theory presented throughout the book. These sections offer insights into sentence structure, grammar, style and clarity.
- Use the sentence models – examine the sentence models provided. Pay attention to their structure, word choice and overall effectiveness.
- Apply to your writing – use the theory and models as inspiration to craft your sentences.
- Remember – writing is a skill that can be honed with practice and guidance. By utilising *Sentence Models for Non-fiction Writing*, your students will be well equipped to write with clarity, precision and impact.

In this book, instead of separating sentence models into writing outcomes, such as newspaper articles, sports reports, book reviews, etc., I've split the sentence models into informative and persuasive writing. Instructions, a biography or a magazine piece on Ancient Egypt are all types of writing where we are trying to inform the reader; therefore, the sentence models can easily be adapted to their outcome. Again, with persuasive writing, you will find many sentence models that can be used to write a discursive essay or an advert, as they share many of the same writing qualities.

I have applied sentence models to different writing outcomes or content in the book, but many can easily be applied to another genre. For example, a pattern of three sentences written to persuade the reader, such as 'Stylish, sleek, safe – the new family car from Japan', could easily be adapted for a biography: 'Determined, brave, resolute – Nelson Mandela was a man to be reckoned with.' A sentence used to write a persuasive advert, 'Not every supermarket cares about their customers like we do,' might be adapted for an informative text about an animal: 'Not every snake is deadly, but the black mamba is a highly venomous killer.'

You can play with the sentence structures and change the content to suit your purpose, but most of all you should encourage your young writers to play with their writing, experiment, and develop a love of language.

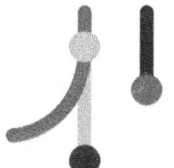

Chapter 2
Why do we write?

Writing is talking to someone else on paper.
William Zinsser (1976)

If you ask a student in your school, 'Why do you write?' then their honest answer should be because my teacher makes me. Ask a teacher why they read their students' writing; the honest answer is, 'It's my job. I have a mortgage to pay.'

This artificial relationship between the writer and the audience is unavoidable in schools. And yes, I am being facetious when I mention the impending mortgage payments, as I'm sure there isn't a teacher alive who chose this profession for the bumper bonuses. When we chose to teach, we did so because we wanted to make a difference in our students' lives: to inspire them, to help them learn, but reality has a way of smacking us around the face with a wet fish when we are faced with a pile of eighty-plus essays on the Industrial Revolution to mark.

What is writing actually for? The common answer is communication, but I get to communicate all the time. Most of my day is spent communicating as a parent, as an educator or as a colleague. Writing something down is a choice not just to communicate but to speak to a wider audience. It's a choice to try to make your thoughts and ideas last. It's a way of creatively expressing ourselves. Capturing our feelings through a poem to a loved one or song lyrics about why your wife left you, helps you express your emotions in a way that moves beyond talking to someone about it. When we write, we don't capture how people speak. If I see a beautiful sunset, I may say, 'That's nice!' I have never seen a sunset and said, 'Look at that azure expanse painted with hues of lilac and amethyst.' It is the same for non-fiction writing. Our patterns of speech are completely different from the written word.

Most days, I open up the website of a popular newspaper and read some of the articles written there, and I can suddenly find myself becoming passionately involved in a world I know nothing about. At breakfast, I discuss with my wife over my cornflakes the decline of the bees in our gardens or the inner workings of a submarine in distress in a far-off ocean. Much like stories, an author's non-fiction writing can take us into different worlds and subjects we had never heard of before.

To understand why we write, we must first understand why we read. For as long as humans have been able to make marks on the ground, we have read. Read to learn, escape our lives, grow as people, and read to entertain ourselves. Yet, when teaching writing, we often forget about this vitally important part of the deal – the reader. Remember that our students always have a guaranteed reader – us, their teachers – but once our writers move away from their guaranteed audience, they move into a world where their reader has no obligation to read a single word. They move into a world where we are awash with the written word. Every day, 2 to 3 million news articles are written, over 300 billion emails are sent, and 500 million tweets are tweeted (or Xs are Xd?). The amount of written content being produced is staggering, and if we want to teach our students to write in a manner that demonstrates clarity of thought, precision and style, then ensuring they are well versed in non-fiction writing is vital.

● Why do we write non-fiction?

Four thousand years ago, the scribes of Ancient Sumeria (modern-day southern Iraq) were tasked with recording on clay tablets the written laws of their society, known as the Code of Ur-Nammu. These clay tablets are one of the earliest known written records, but they are not unique. Throughout history, humans have been recording, from the Anglo-Saxon monks compiling the historical records of their time in the *Anglo-Saxon Chronicle* to the Roman author Pliny the Elder, who wrote about various subjects, ranging from astronomy to natural history. Since humans began to form societies, we have seen different cultures trying to record their culture, laws, history and thoughts about the planet on which we all live. Although these writings come from different eras and different countries and are written in different scripts, they all share a commonality in that, as humans, we have the desire to capture our thoughts, to persuade, to argue, to moan (the Venerable Bede, I'm looking at you here), to gossip, to rant, but most of all to express our humanity by communicating with others.

Now, this all sounds exciting and inspiring, but how does this work when faced with the reality of a class of students? To start, get your students to think about the reasons we may choose to write non-fiction:

1. to think about a subject
2. to express an opinion
3. to teach
4. to persuade
5. to cement knowledge.

Ask them what non-fiction piece they last read and where it fits into this list. You may have a student claim they haven't read any non-fiction, but that's because they may only think of the traditional print media and forget about the endless content they digest online. Once you have got your students to think about why they might want to write – their purpose – then they need to think about the content.

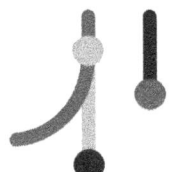 

Chapter 3
Content is king – what shall we write about?

One of the hardest decisions we make for our non-fiction writing is choosing the topic we ask our students to write about. As educators, we want to ensure that we pitch our writing topics so that they engage students, tap into their passions and allow creativity. However, there are also times when we want them to write to demonstrate their learning and knowledge about a subject.

Over the years, I have attempted to tap into my students' passions by letting them choose their own topics. One student wrote an amazing informational text about their passion for tropical fish. Yet, I've also seen students tell me they will write about cats, the life of Bruce Lee or how much they hate mosquitoes only to be presented with a blank page or several paragraphs copied straight from Wikipedia.

I've seen students at the end of a history unit in Year 5 write incredible and moving essays on the Windrush generation. I've also seen a disastrous Year 6 attempt to write informative texts about Sir Walter Raleigh's importation of potatoes. However, I suspect this was a desperate attempt by a Year 6 teacher to include one of the Year 5 and 6 statutory spelling words, 'yacht', as the piece described Raleigh's ship as 'Sir Walter Raleigh's Potato Yacht'.

Giving students free rein over the choice of topic or choosing it from the knowledge you have built up with them in class is not one that directly leads to great writing outcomes. One is not inherently better than the other. I have seen fantastic writing both from a strict writing brief and from students given free rein, but I have also seen students submit identical pieces from a strict brief and pages of waffle with free rein. Ideally, whichever choice we make gives them a passion to write about the subject creatively. To do this well, we must think deeply about how we set our students up to tackle the task rather than simply give them a writing brief.

Most importantly, we must always return to our audience and purpose.

● Audience and purpose

I know I joked in chapter 2 that the audience for our budding writers is their teacher, and a student's purpose for writing is 'My teacher makes me', but this is even more reason to help your young writers move beyond this practical view by answering two questions:

1. Who is my audience?
2. What is my purpose for writing?

Let's start with two definitions for these ideas:

1. Audience – who am I writing for? Who am I targeting my writing at? What age is my audience? What are they interested in? What would they expect from this piece?
2. Purpose – why am I writing this? (E.g. to persuade someone, to explain something to my reader, to make my reader laugh.)

These two choices must sit at the forefront of the writing planning process. The vocabulary we choose, the sentence structures we use, the tone and style of the piece, the form it will take (e.g. monologue, discursive piece), how the piece is put together (composition) are all informed by our audience and our purpose for writing, and this must transfer into our students' planning and writing of a piece.

For example:

Writing a commentary for a David Attenborough nature show

- Audience: people who are interested in the natural world.
- Purpose: to inform them about different habitats and creatures, and entertain them with interesting facts.

Once you have chosen your audience, then this can affect not only your word choices but also your sentence structures. For example, a YouTube audience may want their sentences on how to play a Roblox game with lots of direct address, imperative verbs and short, snappy sentences. In contrast, a manual on quantum physics may be written with many complex sentences and technical, topic-specific vocabulary.

A tip on choosing our audience age: when getting students to think about the age of their audience, the reality is that it is hard for many younger students to write for an audience older than they are because they may not possess the vocabulary or knowledge to do so. It is also a factor that we may not want our students to write for a younger audience, as by doing so they may not show us the appropriate level of writing for their age group.

A quick note on hybrid texts: you may have noticed that recently, in publishing, the lines between the world of fiction and non-fiction have become blurred. Story-writing elements are often woven into a non-fiction text. For example, in an informative text about the Amazon rainforest, you could find a narrative section from an explorer's first-person point of view. Some people refer to this as 'faction' (fact/fiction). You will also see informative texts with a single persuasive paragraph or instructional writing plonked in the middle. This can be embraced in your classrooms to foster independent writing ideas and to stretch your writers by offering more independent choices. Together, we may be working towards a discursive piece on a smoking ban, but ask your young writers what other purposeful paragraph or section they want to add in. What about a persuasive paragraph from the child of a smoker? Or a quick history of the tobacco industry?

● Curse of the expert

The term 'curse of the expert', also known as the 'curse of knowledge', was coined in a 1989 *Journal of Political Economy* article by economists Camerer, Loewenstein and Weber. The curse of knowledge is the idea that there is a cognitive bias when an individual talks to (or teaches) others, which leads us to believe everyone has the same background knowledge. I know I have been guilty of this when teaching. My presumptions of a student's or my class's background knowledge have caused them to struggle to learn something or compounded their misconceptions.

I have encountered this many times over my career. I still remember the confusion in a Year 6 SAT reading paper over a description of camping weather (it was raining). Those students who'd never been camping failed to pick up on the inference. Or the student who was very confused when discussing *Animal Farm*; I found out that she'd never seen a pig. For every student who holidays in the Maldives, we have many more who've never been to the seaside.

I have seen the idea of the curse of the expert used in education primarily to describe teachers when teaching. However, this idea also applies to our young writers. Here's an example:

> Loot llamas are all over the island, so grab them before anyone else if you want new skins and don't want to spend those V-bucks.

Now, you may well recognise the terms 'loot', 'llamas', 'skins' and 'V-bucks' as coming from the popular online game *Fortnite*. However, many of us have no idea what they refer to. This young writer is suffering from the curse of knowledge. They have presumed that their audience has the knowledge that they have about *Fortnite* and, therefore, their writing suffers accordingly. Discussing audience and purpose at the forefront of your writing unit would remedy this. Making it clear that your audience knows nothing about the subject and that your purpose is to inform them about it would help enormously.

The opposite of this problem is when we give an open non-fiction writing task and you have students who have no idea what to write. I worked with a student who, for a comparative writing task, had to write about his dream job. For various reasons, this student knew nothing about the subject and had no idea what he wanted to be. This was unlike another student in my class whose parents were doctors, as he had a much clearer vision of his future. The first student wrote about being a chicken farmer because he liked chickens. The problem was that he needed to learn (as did I!) what the profession of chicken farming entailed. By giving open-ended writing choices, we may instantly disadvantage students in our class, and the task becomes a barrier to their writing. We must remember that for every student with vast knowledge and a particular passion for a subject, we have others whose world experience is limited.

We can consider these two factors to be on a scale.

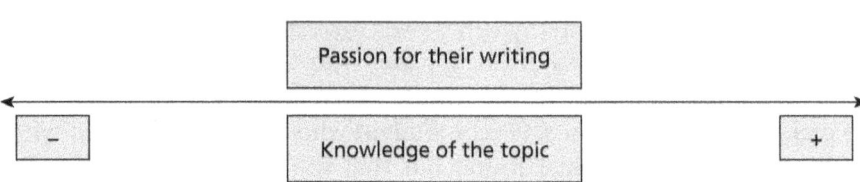

For the writing to be as successful as possible, we must ensure that the *passion* and the *knowledge* are as far on the plus side of the scale as possible. The issue with this is that it's much harder than it looks to do this for thirty-plus students in your class.

Another key aspect is ensuring we have a good spread of content the students write about. I understand that a way of tapping into a student's passion, building global citizenship and relevance to their writing is by asking them to write about current issues such as pollution, or we may tap into areas that many of them are interested in, such as animals. But we should not ask them to write the same piece yearly. These informative, persuasive or discursive writing opportunities are great. As an English lead, I get the chance to have an overview of each year group's writing and often see a lot of repetition of writing content ideas, such as an informative piece on badgers in Year 1, foxes in Year 2, owls in Year 3, etc. This must be designed carefully and intentionally; otherwise, we risk the jam-sandwich syndrome. This is where we see the writing instructions of a Year 6 class and the learning looks no different from the Year 1 class, which is writing instructions on making jam sandwiches. In other words, there is no progression in the knowledge needed, the vocabulary used, the sentence structures or the composition, and both Year 1 and Year 6 students end up writing, '1) First you need to get some bread.'

Another important consideration is picking a topic that is just too hard. If the required knowledge to write about the topic is too great on the scale for the majority of your students, then the writing will suffer. A common reason for difficult content is that teachers try to make the writing outcomes fit their topics. For example, a Year 3 class learning about the Tudors is then asked to write a discursive essay entitled 'Henry VIII was a good king'. Now, if your history unit was sequenced around a series of lessons on what it means to be a good or bad king, then perhaps they will be able to write about this subject, but if you've learned the names of his wives through song, built a Tudor house out of a cereal box and made a golden crown, then this learning is not going to apply. Working with schools, I see writing topics given to young students that many adults would struggle to sit down and write about at length. We must put ourselves in the shoes of our young writers (not literally) and consider the pinch points of the subject we are asking them to write about. Where will they struggle? For example, I am sure that for the Henry VIII piece, they can say he had two of his wives' heads chopped off, so he's bad, but could they get into the topic with the depth to construct an opinion?

This is not to say that we shouldn't grab the opportunity to ask our students to write about a topic they are studying in school. If your writing uses the knowledge you build in your class, it levels the playing field for all your students. A quick practical point on this: I've seen year groups launch into non-fiction writing at the same time that they begin to learn the content of what they are about to write. I'd always start with your fiction unit, start teaching the non-fiction content in your wider curriculum lessons, and then tackle the writing once they've learned it.

All writing is ultimately a question of solving a problem. It may be a problem of where to obtain the facts or how to organise the material.

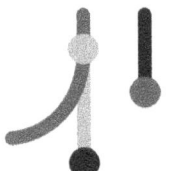 

Chapter 4
Finding the right words – audience and purpose

● Introduction

When thinking about the words I will use in my writing, I first consider the audience (the prime minister or the parents in my school) and my purpose for writing (why I am writing and what I want to achieve – instructing someone in how to cook a risotto or persuading teenagers to use social media less). Knowing the audience and purpose will also affect the level of formality of the writing. My letter to the prime minister may be formal (depending on the prime minister in charge at the time!), whereas my appeal to teenagers may be informal. Again, this will affect my vocabulary choices and my sentence structures.

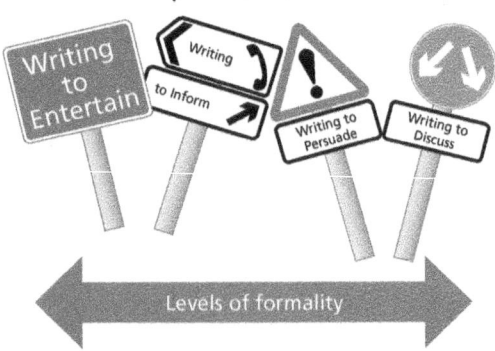

To explain this, I often show my class a short passage such as the one below.

▶ Application to NASA to join a moon landing

I think I should be the boss to fly the space thingie, and when we get there we will plop onto it. It will be hard as there will be massive pebbles and big holes. There is other dangerous stuff as well.

As my audience is NASA and my purpose is to get a job on the rocket's crew, has this piece done the job? Is it formal enough? Have I used the correct technical terminology? Do I sound like I know what I'm talking about?

Here is a quick guide to language choices when wanting to sound more formal:

- Formal vocabulary – avoid slang, contractions (like 'won't' instead of 'will not') and informal expressions (like 'thingie' instead of specific items).
- Precise language – use clear and concise language that avoids ambiguity.
- Formal transitions – use formal transitions like 'however', 'furthermore' and 'consequently' to connect your ideas.

Another great way of grabbing your audience's attention is using the active voice rather than the passive. Sentences in the passive voice can be harder to comprehend.

▶ Passive voice

A huge mistake was made by the referee during the football match.

▶ Confusing because

It focuses on the action being done to the referee, and the mistake is placed at the front of the sentence rather than the referee.

▶ Active voice

The referee made a huge mistake during the match.

Clearer because

It identifies the responsible party – the referee – and focuses on the action performed by the subject (referee).

Using the passive voice can also place a barrier between you as the writer and your audience. The result is a feeling of detachment and a lack of immediacy.

Passive voice

The unsuspecting seal was being stalked by a great white shark. The seal's death was soon to be delivered by the powerful jaws of the shark.

Active voice

The great white shark stalked the unsuspecting seal. With a burst of speed, the shark surged towards the seal, and its powerful jaws sank into the poor creature's side.

See how the active voice version brings the scene to life.

Note that there are times when we need to use the passive voice. For example:

Passive voice

The bank was robbed in the early hours of the morning by the armed suspects.

Active voice

The armed suspects robbed the bank in the early hours of the morning.

The passive voice sentence works better in this context (journalistic writing), as the sentence focuses on the bank being robbed and we do not know who the robbers are.

Another example may depend on your purpose for writing:

Passive voice

Pluto, the dwarf planet at the edge of our solar system, was discovered on 18 February 1930, by Clyde Tombaugh, an American astronomer working at the Lowell Observatory in Arizona.

This example works well if your focus is on the dwarf planet Pluto. However, you may be writing about the person who discovered Pluto. In that case, for this purpose, you should swap it around:

▶ **Active voice**

Clyde Tombaugh, an American astronomer at the Lowell Observatory in Arizona, discovered Pluto on 18 February 1930.

Now, Clyde Tombaugh is at the start of the sentence and this moves your reader's focus onto him.

● Speeding things up and slowing them down

An aspect of non-fiction writing rarely discussed is an author's choice to speed up information or slow it down for their reader. This can be linked to the techniques discussed above using the active and passive voice, but to grab your reader's attention there are other ways that we can slow the writing down. Let's look at an example by imagining we are going to write a biography of the American gymnast Simone Biles:

▶ **Simone Biles**

Born in Columbus, Ohio, in 1997, she began her gymnastics journey at a young age and quickly rose to prominence. With a record-breaking 39 Olympic and World Championship medals, Biles is the most decorated gymnast in history.

You can see that this is very quick-paced and jumps through her life in two sentences. We can slow the writing down at any point we want by using some techniques usually found in narrative writing:

- action – use the active voice to describe things happening
- description – describe people, objects, settings, etc.
- introspection – capture the main character's (subject of the writing) thoughts and feelings
- dialogue.

Now, let's choose an important part of her life story and slow everything down for the reader:

> The arena was a maelstrom of noise. Simone stood at the edge of the mat. 'Will I land it, or will I fall?' she wondered. Her heart pounded against her ribs. With a deep breath, she launched herself into the air, her body twisting and turning with breathtaking precision. Time seemed to slow as she executed her final rotation, a perfect double-back dismount that landed her softly on the mat. A hush fell over the crowd as the judges' scores flashed on the screen – a perfect ten. The roar that erupted was deafening, a tidal wave of sound that carried her away on a wave of euphoria.

By using narrative elements, we have slowed time down to capture our reader. If then we want to snap back into a more traditional, sped-up retelling of her life, we can add a sentence at the end, such as this:

> But what led the great gymnast to this point in her life? Born in…

This can also be used in other forms of non-fiction writing. For example, if you are writing an informative piece on cobras, you could slow things down to write about a cobra attack:

> A hiss filled the jungle air. Eyes as black as the heart of night fixed upon its prey, the cobra coiled, its hood spread in a menacing fan. With lightning speed, it launched itself forward. Its head high, fangs gleaming, the cobra struck.

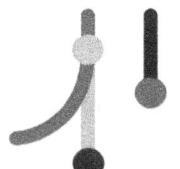 

Chapter 5
Clarity –
making your thinking clear

A common mistake in class is writing driven by the teacher's success criteria or checklist. Students struggle through the task, carefully ensuring that they've started sentences with subordination, three complex sentences, 'up levelled' vocabulary and coordinating conjunctions until they end up with a big word salad that, to all intents and purposes, lets their teacher highlight their assessments to say they have hit their targets, but makes no sense for their reader. All clarity of thought is lost. I have often asked students what they are trying to say in their writing. They stare at me blankly with their eyes twitching to a large piece of flipchart paper on which are written the ten things they need to include, before the student slowly blinks and says that they have no idea what they are trying to say. They've become so tangled up in the checklist that they haven't thought about what they want to communicate.

Many style guides on writing will state that the secret of good writing is to simplify everything. Their tips are eliminating unnecessary words, replacing long words with shorter ones, avoiding adverbs that repeat the verb's meaning, and using the active voice to clarify who is doing what. Now, all of this is true, but it is also true that we need to model, encourage and foster more independence of thought in what students are trying to be clear about.

Here's an example:

> Because African elephants live in Africa, they have big ears. Finally, the elephants like to eat grass. Meanwhile, some other elephants eat 100 kg a day.

You could happily tick off from your checklist: fronted subordination, fronted adverbials and varied sentence openers, but this is not a clear or logically written piece of writing. As a result, the writing is hard to follow. Even without the clumsy writing techniques, we might end up overwriting our non-fiction pieces like this (thanks, ChatGPT!):

> Elephants, those majestic and colossal pachyderms of unparalleled grandeur, possess a remarkable enigma that elicits profound awe from the deepest recesses of one's consciousness. Their sheer enormity, that titanic embodiment of terrestrial majesty, invokes an existential contemplation, an exercise in cerebral gymnastics, causing a momentary suspension of one's cognitive faculties as they confront the awe-inspiring intricacies of this magnificent leviathan. From their massive and intricately corrugated dermal landscape, evoking a geological tapestry of wrinkles, to their remarkably elongated proboscis, a sinuous appendage that defies the very laws of biomechanical physics, elephants represent the epitome of cryptic biological splendour, an inscrutable enigma that beckons the ruminative observer to embark upon an intellectual odyssey to fathom their profound profundity.

William Zinsser (1976) explains this perfectly in his book *On Writing Well*, 'It won't do to say that the reader is too dumb or too lazy to keep pace with the train of thought. If the reader is lost, it's usually because the writer hasn't been careful enough.'

A lack of clarity in our writing can occur because of several factors:

1. The sentence does not follow any logic, e.g. 'Because African elephants live in Africa, they have big ears.' The conclusion does not follow the statement, as the two ideas are unrelated.
2. Sentence ambiguity – meaning the sentence could be misconstrued or read in several ways, confusing the reader.
3. A lack of grammatical control, such as tense slips.

4   Use of words that don't have the correct meaning or are unnecessarily complicated when a simpler word would do the job.

Zinsser describes this problem perfectly:

> Writers must therefore constantly ask: what am I trying to say? Surprisingly often they don't know. Then they must look at what they have written and ask: have I said it? Is it clear to someone encountering the subject for the first time? If it's not, some fuzz has worked its way into the machinery. The clear writer is someone clearheaded enough to see this stuff for what it is: fuzz.
>
> Zinsser, *On Writing Well* (1976)

Chapter 6
The 'problem' with English

While living in Thailand many years ago, I took Thai language lessons. Once I got to grips with the major differences of learning a tonal language (it can be embarrassing when the same word can mean 'horse', 'come' and 'prostitute'), I began to marvel at the simplicity of the sentence structures.

Let's look at the example of asking in Thai 'Where is the toilet?' – 'Hong nam yuu thi nai?' This roughly translates as 'Toilet is where?' Before I mustered up the courage to try out my new language skills in public, I would often end up hearing myself asking a local, 'Excuse me, sorry to bother you, I don't suppose if you'd mind pointing me in the right direction of the toilet please?' and inwardly wince at how convoluted I was making such a simple question. Although English can become overly heavy on complex sentence structures, it's not the only language to do so. Spanish often has multiple subordinate clauses in one sentence, Dutch sentences can have many prepositions in one sentence, and German has long compound words and embedded clauses. Each language has its quirks of grammar and rules built up over hundreds of years. But I will presume that we teach our students to write non-fiction texts in English and look at some particular points to pay attention to with our grammar system.

In English, we use three main types of sentences: simple, compound and complex.

▶ Simple

She kicked the football.

▶ **Compound**

She kicked the football and scored a goal.

▶ **Complex**

Despite the pressure from the defender, she kicked the football and scored a goal.

Our problem in teaching writing is that we often push for complex sentences from our students without them knowing the purpose. I have seen many lessons where students must create complex sentences using connectors from word lists. These are often used incorrectly and without thought, and you end up with sentences like this:

Moreover, from the pressure from the defender, she scored a goal.

or

She ran down the wing. Meanwhile, she kicked the ball and scored a goal.

This is not to say that we want our students to always write in Hemingwayesque simple sentences, as transitional words and phrases help us connect ideas and ensure cohesion (a smooth flow). Transitional words help to guide our readers through our thoughts, making them easier to follow and comprehend. Transitions can also show relationships between ideas, such as contrast, addition, cause and effect, sequence, etc.

Here are some common types of transitions and examples of each:

▶ **Addition**

and, also, furthermore, moreover, in addition, besides

▶ **Contrast**

but, however, on the other hand, nevertheless, yet, although

▶ **Cause and effect**

because, since, therefore, thus, consequently, as a result

▶ **Comparison**

similarly, likewise, in the same way

▶ **Sequence/order**
first, next, then, finally, subsequently

▶ **Emphasis**
indeed, in fact, certainly, truly

▶ **Example/illustration**
for example, for instance, such as, namely

▶ **Summary/conclusion**
in conclusion, to sum up, therefore, in summary, thus

▶ **Clarification**
in other words, that is to say, to clarify, specifically

In summary, transitions make the links and joins between our ideas smooth and easier to follow. As I write this book, I currently live and work in Taiwan, where Mandarin Chinese is the main language. Like sentences in many languages, Chinese sentences typically end when the meaning is complete. Chinese relies heavily on context, meaning and syntax rather than strict punctuation rules to indicate the end of a sentence. This means the sentence ends once the intended message is conveyed clearly and completely. The structure and flow of Chinese sentences can vary, but clarity of meaning is always the primary goal. In English, this is different as it is our grammar system that mostly decides when the sentence should come to a stop. In Chinese we don't even have tenses to contend with. Instead, the context will often imply when an action took place. The result of this in English is that those transitions are vital to our writing and spoken language.

Let's look at two examples from an essay about Emily Brontë's *Wuthering Heights* to illustrate this point.

▶ **Without transitions**

The relationship between Heathcliff and Catherine Earnshaw is a central theme driving the narrative. Their connection is deeply intertwined with the harsh landscape of the Yorkshire moors. Their affair is fraught with passion and leads to their destruction.

Catherine's declaration 'I am Heathcliff' epitomises their bond. Their love is also marked by betrayal, jealousy and revenge, leading to tragic consequences for themselves and those around them.

▶ Added transitions

In Emily Brontë's *Wuthering Heights*, the relationship between Heathcliff and Catherine Earnshaw is a central theme driving the narrative. **Throughout** the book, their connection is deeply intertwined with the harsh landscape of the Yorkshire moors. Their affair is fraught with passion**; however,** it ultimately destroys them. Catherine's declaration 'I am Heathcliff' epitomises their bond. **Yet,** their love is also marked by betrayal, jealousy and revenge, leading to tragic consequences for themselves and those around them.

Adding transitions helps the reader follow the writer's train of thought.

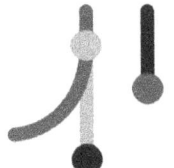 

Chapter 7
Writing to inform – explaining it properly

The most common non-fiction writing is about informing your reader. There are many sub-genres, such as reports, instructional writing, technical writing, biographies, journalistic writing and expository writing. Each of these must be tailored to the audience and your purpose for writing.

One aspect of informative writing that students struggle with the most is explaining the information properly. Let me show you an example. In my class, we wrote biographies of Neil Armstrong. To do this, we researched his life, and the students made some bullet point notes like those below about the different periods of his life.

▶ **Test pilot and military pilot career**
- Neil fought in the Korean War and flew 78 combat missions.
- Neil nearly died when his plane hit an anti-aircraft cable.
- Neil became a test pilot at the National Advisory Committee for Aeronautics (NACA).
- Neil accidentally flew the world's fastest plane (the X-15) into space.

Chapter 7 Writing to inform – explaining it properly

The issue here is when the student ends up rewriting their bullet-pointed notes into a facsimile of the original bullet points:

> *Neil Armstrong fought in the Korean War and flew 78 daring combat missions. He then became a test pilot at NACA, where he narrowly escaped a collision with an anti-aircraft cable. Neil accidentally piloted the X-15 rocket plane to the edge of space.*

Now, common feedback on this would be to add cohesion by using fronted adverbials, and you'd end up with a paragraph like this one:

> *In 1951, Neil Armstrong was deployed in the Korean War, flying a staggering 78 combat missions. Following his service, he transitioned to NACA as a test pilot, where he narrowly avoided a harrowing collision with an anti-aircraft cable. In another remarkable feat, Armstrong even accidentally piloted the X-15 rocket plane to the edge of space.*

What's missing now is a sub-heading to orient the reader and a topic sentence to introduce the paragraph.

▶ A pilot's life for me

> *After university, Neil Armstrong gained invaluable experience as a pilot through a series of remarkable challenges. In 1951, Neil Armstrong was deployed in the Korean War, flying a staggering 78 combat missions. Following his service, he transitioned to NACA as a test pilot, where he narrowly avoided a harrowing collision with an anti-aircraft cable. In another remarkable feat, Armstrong even accidentally piloted the X-15 rocket plane to the edge of space.*

Now, this is certainly improved, but there is another option. Instead of four chronologically driven facts that whizz through this period of his life, you can model how to take one exciting incident in detail, such as his testing of the world's fastest plane (X-15), and then write about this information in depth.

▶ A pilot's life for me

> *After university, Neil Armstrong gained invaluable experience as a pilot through a series of remarkable challenges. One particularly*

exciting story involves his X-15 rocket plane flight on 30 November 1960. When an engine malfunction threw the craft off course, Armstrong faced a baptism by fire. This threw off the aircraft's balance and caused it to veer off course into the edge of space. Neil reached an altitude of 48,840 feet. As Armstrong regained control, he began his descent, and the X-15 re-entered the Earth's atmosphere at an extreme angle. This caused the craft to skip off the atmosphere like a flat stone on water, bouncing violently several times. The g-forces inside the cockpit were immense, nearly causing him to black out. Through sheer skill and determination, Armstrong regained control and brought the X-15 back to a safe landing at Edwards Air Force Base. Though shaken by the experience, he emerged unharmed.

The immediacy and excitement in this informative paragraph use more detail and present a more in-depth look at one incident to engage the reader.

We can see the same problem with other informative writing, such as this piece on crocodiles. A student's plan and paragraph may look like this:

Research notes:

- *Crocodiles can live up to 80 years old.*
- *Crocodiles mostly live off fish.*
- *Crocodiles use their powerful jaws to catch their prey.*

Amazingly, crocodiles can live up to 80 years old. They mostly live off fish. These amazing beasts use their powerful jaws to catch their prey.

Again, we have a short paragraph that regurgitates the bullet points. Instead, we can model how to choose just one of the points and explain it properly and in depth. For this example, let's focus on how a crocodile hunts.

▶ Expert hunters

Crocodiles are stealthy hunters. They patiently wait for prey to come close, then launch a surprise attack with their powerful bodies and bone-crushing bite. Once clamped on, the crocodile utilises its signature death roll, spinning rapidly to disorient and drown its prey. Since they can't chew, they rely on this drowning tactic and the water's environment to weaken and tear apart their food before swallowing it whole.

A quick topic sentence and one of the topics explored in depth are more interesting for the reader and make it easier for the student to master the knowledge before writing. Getting them to learn about one aspect and discuss it with a partner or give a quick speech to the class helps with that oral rehearsal of what they will write.

▶ In summary

Paragraph style one: topic sentence, followed by four related points around that area, concluding sentence.

An example for paragraph one would be an informative text about crocodiles and a section on diet/food, etc. The topic sentence might be followed by a point on what they eat, what sort of diet they have, where they catch their food and if different species have different diets.

Paragraph style two: topic sentence, followed by four more closely related points and drill down into the subject matter in detail, concluding sentence.

An example for paragraph two would have a section on how crocodiles hunt, which would have four parts detailing in depth the process, e.g. what they eat, where and how they catch it in detail: the way they enter the water, how their jaws clamp around their prey, how they use their bodies to twist in the water and drown their victim, etc.

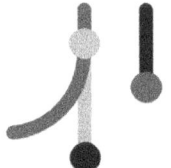 

Chapter 8
Sentence models to inform

In this chapter, I have collected lots of sentences that can be modelled, taught and used by students when they want to inform their readers. As discussed in chapter 1, you may find that the sentence model can also be applied to other types of non-fiction writing. I advise playing around with the sentence structures with your class and seeing what magic happens!

WHAT? + 'IS'

This is a summary sentence that sits at the start of a paragraph to clarify the information that will be discussed in detail.

> A volcano is an opening in the Earth's crust through which molten rock, ash and gases erupt.

STATEMENT + 'THIS' + MORE INFORMATION

> Theropods walked on two legs. This group included the T-Rex.

STATEMENT + 'ING' FORM EXPLANATION

> The heart is the hardest working muscle, beating 100,000 times a day.

STATEMENT + 'THAT' + 'ING' FORM EXPLANATION

> Tsunamis are large waves that rush across the ocean, causing terrible damage when they hit the shore.

STATEMENT '– IN FACT' + STATEMENT

> Albert Einstein was a famous scientist – in fact, one of the most famous people in the world.

STATEMENT – MORE INFORMATION

Blood is made of plasma – a mixture of proteins, salts and hormones.

▶ Anadiplosis

Make a statement. Start the next sentence with the same word or phrase (adds cohesion and explains more).

Neil Armstrong set off to space on a rocket. This rocket was called Apollo 11.

All matter is made up of particles called atoms. Atoms make up everything around us in the observable universe.

STATEMENT + VERB + ACTION

The saltwater crocodile is a ferocious predator. Swimming at speeds of nearly 20 mph, around three times faster than humans.

STATEMENT + 'THIS' + MORE INFORMATION

An ostrich's heart has four chambers. This type of heart is a well-adapted organ that allows these large birds to meet the demands of their active lifestyle.

WITH + STATEMENT

With nearly 50 national parks, Canada has an abundance of nature to choose from.

WHERE? to WHERE? + WHAT?

Taiwan has everything from the rugged east coast to the sparkling beaches on the south coast.

▶ Appositive and reverse appositive

An appositive is a noun or noun phrase that sits beside another noun or noun phrase to identify or rename it. It provides more information about the first noun and adds detail or clarification to the sentence.

NOUN + NOUN PHRASE

The *Titanic*, the grandest luxury ship ever built, sailed across the Atlantic Ocean.

Sentence Models for Non-fiction Writing

NOUN PHRASE + NOUN

The grandest luxury ship ever built, the *Titanic*, was sailing across the Atlantic Ocean.

'Like' can be used to paint a clearer picture for the reader. A well-chosen simile helps the reader picture what is being described.

NOUN + WHAT IT'S LIKE

The Apollo 11 rocket was like a long, thin metal pencil.

QUANTIFIERS – 'EVERY', 'SOME', 'A FEW', 'MANY'

Some careful work here with your class is helpful, so they have the prerequisite knowledge to explain something correctly. For example, you don't want to say 'Dinosaurs were carnivorous', as some were not. Instead, you can quantify your statement with 'Some dinosaurs were carnivorous'.

Quantifiers can also be used to great effect to make comparisons.

OPPOSITES – [QUANTIFER + STATEMENT] ×2

Some dinosaurs were carnivorous, but most were thought to be herbivores.

HOW MANY?

Only a few ___

Many ___

A single ___

'SOME ARE' + 'OTHERS ARE'

Some are tiny, and others are enormous.

OPPOSITES

Not every ___

Not all ___

Many ___ don't ___

OPPOSITES (PARALLEL) + 'ING' FORM

Claiming the throne is one thing; keeping it is another.

STATEMENT + 'WHICH' (EXPLAIN)

The king helped his people grow crops, which meant they were well fed and happy.

'WITH' + WHAT?

With this amazing victory, the Allies grew closer to winning the war.

With a flair for drama, he___ .

With a passion for ___ , she ___ .

'ACCORDING TO' + WHAT?

According to legend ___

According to scientists ___

According to experts ___

BIOGRAPHY INFORM

More than anything else, X loved to ___ .

ACTION – VERB + STATEMENT

Dive with the dolphins in the ocean's depths, ride across the desert with the camels, and climb the mountain peaks with the goats.

'AS' + WHAT?

As the Greeks ___ , the ___ .

WHERE? + 'THERE' + WHAT?

The Anglo-Saxons settled in ___ . There they ___ .

Napoleon was exiled to the isle of Elba. There he ___ .

'FROM' (EXTREMES/OPPOSITES)

From a humble village to a mighty city. Athens's mighty rise...

DOUBLE ADJECTIVE

Strong and majestic eagles can be seen soaring through our skies.

SHOW IMPORTANCE – 'WITHOUT' + WHAT?

Without trees, we would lose one of our planet's main supplies of oxygen.

CORRECT A FACT

You might think ___ but ___ .

You may have heard ___ but___ .

You may know ___ but___ .

You may be surprised to know/discover ___

VERB + STATEMENT

Hatched from an egg, baby crocodiles emerge.

STATEMENT + 'IN FACT'

The great white shark has an incredible sense of smell; in fact, they are able to smell 1 millilitre of blood in 1 million millilitres of water.

OPPOSITES + STATEMENT

Spider silk is a true wonder of nature – as strong as steel, as light as a feather.

3 × ACTIONS + STATEMENT

The sky goes dark, the wind picks up, and people run for their lives when a hurricane comes.

WHERE? + WHAT?

In the cool morning air, the ___ .

WHERE? + WHO?

The Amazon rainforest is home to ___ .

WHERE? (ALLITERATIVE) + WHO?

Dry, dusty deserts are the home to ___ .

RULE OF 3 – KEY FEATURES

With their powerful jaws, razor-sharp claws and incredible speed, ___ .

WHAT? + WHERE IT TRAVELS

This can be used to describe blood moving through the human body or the digestive system.

> Blood courses through the body's intricate network of blood vessels, travelling from the heart to the lungs to pick up oxygen, then returning to the heart to be pumped throughout the body, delivering oxygen and nutrients to cells and carrying away waste products.

COMPARE – 'IN SOME CASES' + 'IN OTHER CASES'

> In some cases, owls hunt by sight, using their keen vision to spot prey in the dark, while in other cases, some owl species rely on exceptional hearing to locate their meals.

'WE KNOW' + WHAT?

> We know that ___ .
>
> We know that ___ but ___ .

'FROM' + 'TO' + STATEMENT

> From the depths of the Antarctic Ocean to the mountain peaks of Nepal, our planet is teeming with life.

STATEMENT + 'THIS MEANS'

> Gravity is smaller on the moon. This means you can jump higher there.

QUESTION + ANSWER IT

> Are chickens a direct descendant of dinosaurs? Yes! (*or* The answer is yes!)

2 × 'SOME' + 'OTHERS'

> Some ___ Some ___ Others ___

COMPARE – 'LIKE' + WHAT?

> Like many animals today, dinosaurs travelled the land in search of food.

COMPARE – 'NO' + WHAT?

    No creature had ___ .

    No animal has ever ___ .

HOW OFTEN?

    STATEMENT + Sometimes, ___ .

    STATEMENT + Occasionally, ___ .

LARGE SPAN OF TIME

    For thousands of years,

    Since the dawn of time,

    Since the (last ice age),

    Over the past hundred years,

OVER A SHORTER PERIOD

    During the summer,

    During the war,

RIGHT NOW

    Now,

    At this moment,

    Today,

SPECIFIC TIME/DATE

    One night in 1933,

    On the 14th of September 1986,

    In the 1970s,

    By the 1800s,

WHO? + STATEMENT/COMMAND

    Scientists think ___ .

    Experts think ___ .

SEQUENCE YOUR THOUGHTS

STATEMENT. Then, ___ .

MODALS

Likely, certain, possible, may, etc.

You may encounter bears in the great wilds of Canada.

'IF' CONDITIONAL (END OF THE PARAGRAPH OR PIECE) – FUTURE THINKING

If we continue to destroy our planet ___ .

PREPOSITIONAL PHRASES

START

In the Amazon, ___ .

At university, ___ .

MIDDLE

Neil Armstrong was born in Wapakoneta, Ohio, in 19___ .

USING 'AS' TO ADD MORE INFORMATION

As ___ , ___ .

As part of the digestion process, ___ .

[Technical word], also known as, ___ .

Nitrous oxide, also known as laughing gas, is ___ .

USING 'BY' TO ADD MORE INFORMATION

The great white shark attacks its prey by ___ .

The prey is attacked by the great white shark by ___ .

(The visual model with the shark first is more powerful.)

CONVERSATIONAL

STATE FACT + Yes, that's correct!

Sentence Models for Non-fiction Writing

CONTRADICTION/OPPOSITE

At first ___ + STATEMENT, but ___ .

At first you might think that a slow loris is cute, but it has a venom stored in its elbows that can kill.

STATEMENT + EXPLANATION

An earthquake is ___ + ___ .

An earthquake is the Earth's violent shaking caused by the sudden release of energy in its crust.

Useful explanation vocab: 'caused by', 'created by', 'which is', 'as a result of', 'results from', 'stems from', 'is produced by', 'is triggered by', 'gives rise to', 'because of', 'owing to', 'due to', 'on account of', 'contributes to'.

PATTERNS OF 3

We need it to ___ . We need it to ___ . We need it to ___ .

TIME GENERAL + TIME SPECIFIC

The date was ___ , the time was ___ .

'ONCE' + NOW

Once the area was uninhabitable. Now, there is a giant city that is full of people.

'PEOPLE IN' + WHAT?

People in Denmark are well known for their love of nature.

WHERE? + 'HAS'?

Canada has the most lakes in the world.

WHERE? + 'IS HOME TO?

Russia is home to the largest lake in the world.

WHERE? + 'IS'?

Mali is primarily a desert country.

WHAT? + WHERE? ×3

> In Brazil, music is everywhere. It beats from the samba bars in Rio, it's drummed in the famous carnival and is played on traditional instruments by the indigenous tribes in the Amazon rainforest.

▶ A quick note on superlatives

A superlative is the highest degree of comparison for an adjective or adverb. It describes the most extreme or intense quality of something within a group. Here are some examples:

- adjective:

Positive: big

Comparative: bigger

Superlative: biggest

- adverb:

Positive: quickly

Comparative: more quickly

Superlative: most quickly

Superlatives are often used to emphasise a quality or to make a strong statement and are useful in non-fiction writing.

Example:

> Libya is generally considered the hottest country in the world, with average summer temperatures reaching over 40 degrees Celsius (104 degrees Fahrenheit).

> The Himalayas are the highest and most massive mountain ranges in the world.

INCORRECT IDEA + TRUTH

> People once thought the world was flat. In fact, ___ .

Sentence Models for Non-fiction Writing

THREE-WORD SENTENCE FOR IMPACT

Out in the African savannah, the sun beats down. It is hot. A black mamba slithers across the ground.

'OR' TO COMPARE (GIVE AN EXTRA EXPLANATION OF THE INFORMATION)

The heart's rhythmic pumping action, or heartbeat, is essential for circulating blood around the body.

ONE WORD + STATEMENT/QUESTION

Artificial intelligence. What is it, and why should we care?

History. It's a massive subject!

'ONE OF THE' + WHAT?

One of the most interesting ways ___ .

One of the earliest examples of ___ .

One of the largest ___ .

One of the simplest ___ .

WHO? (PLURAL)

Astronomers believe ___ .

Surfers love ___ .

Tigers are ___ .

WHO? + WHAT? + WHAT?

King Kong has roared and rampaged across our cinema screens since 1933.

TWO NOUNS

The ___ and ___ (the costume and props)

VERB STARTER

Carved by the people of ___

Discovered in ___

PREPOSITION STARTER – WHERE? OR 3 × WHERE?

Deep beneath our feet,

Deep beneath our feet, way underground, in the Earth's centre, you will find the Earth's inner core.

2 × ADVERB

Slowly and steadily, the leopard stalks its prey.

3 × ALLITERATION OR ALLITERATIVE PAIR

The wild wind whips

These majestic mountains

EXPLANATION – 'AS…', …

As food enters the mouth, it is broken down by teeth and saliva, as this mixture moves to the stomach, it is further digested by gastric juices, and, finally, as the digested food reaches the small intestine, nutrients are absorbed into the bloodstream.

'ONE' + STATEMENT

Stating that something or someone is the 'one' or the number one can show their importance.

One scientist ___

One towering mountain ___

One creature ___

DIRECT ADDRESS – COMMAND

Think about ___ .

Imagine that ___ .

STATEMENT + LIST OR LIST + STATEMENT

Mars is a dangerous planet with its: toxic soil, extreme temperatures, violent storms and radiation.

Note – this is a good place to teach a colon list sentence.

With its radiation, violent storms, extreme temperatures and toxic soil, Mars is a dangerous planet.

Use a dash to drop in an extra explanation or information.

STATEMENT – INFORMATION – FINISH STATEMENT

Jupiter's moons – including the colossal Ganymede – are some of the largest moons in our solar system.

STATEMENT + COLON (EXPLAIN FURTHER)

The human body is an engineering wonder: from the microscopic cells and organs to the muscles and bones that allow movement.

'WITH' + STATEMENT

With elongated necks and legs, the giraffe is well suited to its environment.

▶ Sentences to introduce technical vocabulary

Adding tier two or tier three terms can add authorial confidence to your writing.

TECHNICAL NAME + NICKNAME

The deoxyribonucleic acid molecule, or DNA, can be found in all living organisms.

PROPER NOUN NAME + NICKNAME

Edson Arantes do Nascimento, better known as Pelé, was a Brazilian professional footballer.

LATIN NAME + POPULAR NAME

Panthera tigris, or the tiger, is native to Asia.

OTHER NAMES

Don't be fooled by its many aliases (silver lion, mountain lion, cougar) – it's still a puma!

WHAT? OR WHO? 'IS CALLED'

The ___ is called a ___ .

WHAT?/WHO? + 'MORE COMMONLY KNOWN AS' + WHAT?

Edson Arantes do Nascimento, more commonly known as Pelé, was one of the world's most famous footballers.

Grampus whales, more commonly known as orcas, are found ___ .

TECHNICAL WORD + 'IS' + STATEMENT (OPEN THE PARAGRAPH WITH IT)

Global warming is ___ .

'CALLED'/'NAMED'/'KNOWN AS'

Bats use a special technique called echolocation to hunt in the dark.

ADJECTIVE + TECHNICAL WORD + STATEMENT

Intense precipitation ___ .

Aggressive predators ___ .

Lush rainforest ___ .

New technologies ___ .

EXPLAIN THE WORD (TECHNICAL TERM)

The word/name/term ___ comes from ___ which means ___ .

The term 'checkmate' comes from the Persian phrase 'shāh māt', which translates as 'the king is dead'.

The name T-Rex comes from the Greek for 'tyrant lizard' and the Latin word for 'king', which is *rex*.

STATEMENT + PARENTHESES (EXPLAIN FURTHER)

Aeroplanes utilise powerful turbines (jet engines) to propel the aircraft through the sky.

WHAT? + dash to add information

The *Titanic* – a luxurious ocean liner – sank on its maiden voyage in 1912.

Sentence Models for Non-fiction Writing

STATEMENT + FURTHER EXPLANATION

Electric cars use electric motors instead of traditional internal combustion engines. To explain how they work we need to look in more detail at their batteries.

'SOME' + 'SOME' + 'SHARE'

Some of them have faced war. Some of them have faced racism. But they all share one thing: a desire to make their life better.

WHAT? + 'TAKE' + WHAT? + 'FOR A START'

Mars is a dangerous planet. Take its extreme temperature changes for a start.

Mars is a dangerous planet. For a start, take its extreme temperatures.

QUICK LIST OF THREE

Mars is a dangerous planet – extreme temperatures, radiation, toxic soil – and we will have a lot to overcome if we are to colonise it.

SINGLE WORD FOR IMPACT

The Amazon rainforest is full of dangerous creatures, but one creature may be more dangerous than all the others. Mosquitoes.

DOUBLE WORD FOR IMPACT

Travelling up the Amazon river can be treacherous, with clouds of mosquitoes plaguing you at every turn. Very irritating.

▶ The point of a subheading

Subheadings can replace the first statement sentence, meaning you can go straight into the information. For example, in a piece about sea turtles:

What do they eat?

Green turtles can be found munching on algae, seagrasses and seaweed.

▶ Using a caption box

Rather than explain something in your main paragraph, you can make a quick statement in a caption box next to a picture.

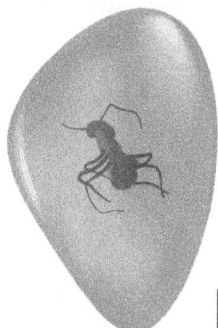

Amber is fossilised tree resin.

Or, here's how _____ (e.g. the lightbulb) works:

1)

2)

3)

▶ Summarizing

THREE-WORD SUMMARY

That really sucks.

(End of paragraph on negative effects of plastic)

That's really amazing.

WRAP IT UP (QUICK SUMMARY OF THE WHOLE TEXT)

Now that you know ___

Now that you know how important it is to look after your body, perhaps you could start by incorporating a healthy diet and regular exercise into your daily routine.

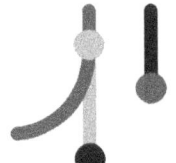 

Chapter 9
Let it flow – cohesion

We have many words in the English language that can link your ideas together: 'but', 'yet', 'however', 'nevertheless', 'still', 'instead', 'thus', 'therefore', 'meanwhile', 'now', 'later', 'today', 'subsequently' and several more. But chucking these in a big list for your students will only lead to clumsy writing. It's like building a house by glueing the walls together with a Pritt stick. Students will invariably chuck 'nevertheless' on to the end of a sentence and, therefore, to a fact that doesn't link. They are not universal linking words and cannot be delivered to students in the same long list.

As discussed earlier, teaching a few linking words and ensuring students know how to use each tool correctly is far more effective. Used well, these links and joins will become invisible to the reader, and only your content or ideas will jump off the page.

Don't forget that sometimes you also want to link your paragraphs. For example:

> *Mae Jemison's most famous achievement was becoming the first African American woman to travel into space. Her historic mission aboard the Space Shuttle Endeavour in 1992 broke barriers and paved the way for other women to pursue careers in science and space exploration.*

Now, if I want to go back and explain her early life, then I can add some cohesion between the paragraphs to orient my reader:

> *Mae Jemison's most famous achievement was becoming the first African American woman to travel into space. Her historic mission aboard the Space Shuttle Endeavour in 1992 broke barriers and paved the way for other women to pursue careers in science and space exploration. But how did she end up becoming an astronaut?*

How does adding this link to the end help me transition into my next paragraph? The easiest links to use are rhetorical questions, but like any new writing technique, once you've taught your students how to do this, they will end every paragraph with a rhetorical question. It's important to show them that these are not the only ways to build links and to think about the overall composition of their writing.

▶ Other ways to link your writing

1. Titles and subheadings.
2. Logical connections.
3. Ensure a smooth flow of ideas – make sure your paragraphs build on each other logically.
4. Avoid abrupt transitions – use transition words and phrases to guide the reader from one idea to the next.
5. Use pronouns – refer to people, places or things mentioned in previous paragraphs.
6. To show addition – 'and', 'also', 'in addition', 'furthermore', 'moreover'.
7. To show contrast – 'but', 'however', 'nevertheless', 'on the other hand'.
8. To show cause and effect – 'because', 'therefore', 'as a result', 'consequently'.
9. To show time – 'then', 'next', 'after', 'finally'.
10. To show examples – 'for example', 'for instance', 'such as'.
11. To summarise – 'in conclusion', 'in summary', 'to sum up'.

Sentence Models for Non-fiction Writing

● More links – sentence openers

One way of linking your writing is to use sentence openers, but sentence openers are not inherently interesting. The content and the ideas in the sentence make a piece interesting (or not) to read. Yet, when teaching non-fiction writing, as a profession we have got hung up on varying our sentence openers without explaining (or knowing) why we do this. Let's look at an example:

▶ Mars – informative text

Mars is the fourth planet from the Sun in our solar system. Mars is named after the Roman god of war. Mars is known as the Red Planet. Mars is red because of the iron oxide in its soil.

Common feedback for a text written this way is that you should vary your sentence openers. Often, you will hear teachers and students state that it's because the repetition of Mars is boring. But what does this mean? Let's vary the openers and see if this idea stands up.

▶ Mars – informative text

Firstly, Mars is the fourth planet from the Sun in our solar system. Secondly, Mars is named after the Roman god of war. Thirdly, it is known as the Red Planet. Lastly, Mars is red because of the iron oxide in its soil.

Each sentence opener is now different. I have varied my openers, but is it more 'interesting'?

Varied openers do make the writing better by the fact of being varied. Telling students to vary their openers is like asking them to 'do it better' without explaining what 'better' is.

Often I see large lists of openers for students to use to vary their writing. A popular teaching resource website has a 'Vary your sentence openers' resource sheet with 54 options. The chances of students who need to add cohesion to their writing picking openers that work is like sticking your finger in the air and making a wish. Many times, you end up with writing like this:

Chapter 9 Let it flow – cohesion

▶ Mars – informative text

Moreover, it is the fourth planet from the Sun in our solar system. Lastly, Mars is named after the Roman god of war. Coincidentally, it is known as the Red Planet. Mars is red because of the iron oxide in its soil.

Let's remind ourselves of what the actual functions of sentence openers are.

● Cohesion

When we hear the term 'cohesion' in writing, it means the flow from sentence to sentence and paragraph to paragraph. A more developed cohesive piece will progress as we expand on points, avoid repetition, establish a viewpoint, and come full circle to the original statement.

One of the main points of sentence openers is not that they make the writing good but that they make it flow. Therefore, they should become invisible. It is much like well-written dialogue in a story where the reader skips the word 'said' as they take in the sentence.

▶ Mars – informative text

Mars is the fourth planet from the Sun in our solar system. Interestingly, Mars is named after the Roman god of war. Also, Mars is known as the Red Planet. Lastly, Mars is red because of the iron oxide in its soil.

Now, it won't win a Pulitzer, and there are flow issues regarding the content. However, at least now, it flows. The reader can take in the facts without the repetitive use of Mars, the clumsy use of 'firstly', 'secondly', 'thirdly' or the completely distracting incorrect use. Why else does this now flow better?

Our brain builds visual models of the sentences it reads. Consider the effort with 'Mars' at the head of each sentence. My brain begins to try to comprehend each fact given with the word 'Mars'. This means we will struggle to take in the information after it as we constantly return to the word 'Mars'. It's become a distraction from the content we were trying to put across.

Another problem with this is that we will take each sentence header (the first word) and our brain will prepare us for the information to be given. Start with the word 'Mars' in the first sentence, then that's great as we have quickly established the content. Start with 'amazingly' and the reader prepares to be amazed. Be careful that the information that follows does amaze your reader. I have never got over the student in my class who, when writing a biography of Neil Armstrong, wrote 'Fun fact – Neil Armstrong's wife died in 2018' (a classic example of the success criteria overruling good decision-making).

● Vary the subject

Let's say we have written an informative piece about tiger sharks. Before writing, I presume students will automatically vary their writing by using synonyms and expanded noun phrases. Instead, we end up with this:

> *Tiger sharks have distinctive dark stripes resembling a tiger's pattern. Tiger sharks are among the most formidable predators in the ocean. Tiger sharks are incredibly powerful swimmers.*

I may then ask students to vary their use of 'tiger sharks' at the start of their sentences. I often see written feedback like this: 'Next step: Vary your sentence openers'. But what does this mean? This presumes they know how and what they can vary them with. This is a classic curse-of-the-expert scenario.

Instead, we could build into our lesson a teaching point in our sequence of lessons before we begin to write. We can make it explicit that we may end up overusing the term 'tiger shark' and can teach them how to replace it with a pronoun, a synonym or an expanded noun phrase. To do this, we can collect quick lists before teaching and contextually cover the grammar that needs to be taught to do this, such as how pronouns function in writing.

- Pronouns: 'it', 'they'.
- Synonyms: 'sea creature', 'creature', 'apex predator'.
- Expanded noun phrases: 'fierce creatures', 'deadly predators', 'toothed terror'.

*Tiger sharks have distinctive dark stripes resembling a tiger's pattern. They are among the most **formidable predators** in the ocean. **These fierce creatures** are incredibly powerful swimmers.*

● The importance of precise expanded noun phrases

Sometimes, we don't just want to use a single word; a precise noun phrase can help bring your writing to life. Rather than repeating 'great white shark', we can build up a quick list of precise noun phrases that can substitute: 'coastal predators', 'expert hunters', 'powerful swimmers', 'deep-sea dwellers', 'silent hunters', etc.

Be careful when letting students loose with the thesaurus to avoid them coming up with phrases such as 'cartilaginous fish with electroreception' or 'resident of the coral reef ecosystem'.

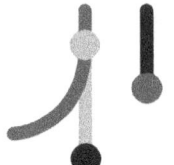 

Chapter 10
The four sentence types – composition

In non-fiction writing, there are four sentence types:
1 **statements** – 'Cakes are made with sugar, flour and eggs.'
2 **questions** – 'Do you like cake?'
3 **exclamations** – 'What a delicious cake!'
4 **commands** – 'Eat your cake.'

Teaching your students these four sentence types is useful for structuring paragraphs and creating cohesion. The crux here is to show how most of our writing is made up of statements, but to create flow we can add questions, commands and exclamations. Let's look at an example:

What an extraordinary medium gaming has become! Video games offer endless possibilities for entertainment and escapism. Whether it's the thrill of competition, the joy of creation or the satisfaction of problem-solving, gaming has something to offer everyone. But what does the world of gaming hold for us next?

This paragraph is built up like this:
- exclamation
- statements
- question.

Chapter 10 The four sentence types – composition

We can show students the different structures that will help them write their own by deconstructing existing non-fiction paragraphs. Often, I will use a paragraph from our text or write a model paragraph on the board. Once I have taught the four sentence types, we can pick the paragraph apart to see what it comprises. When your students learn how to deconstruct and see the paragraph structure, they can begin constructing their own paragraphs. Students who read a lot of non-fiction will have picked up the style and sentence types without realising it, but it doesn't hurt all writers to think about their craft more intentionally.

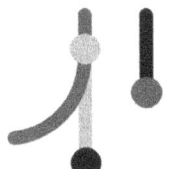 

Chapter 11
Writing to persuade – the flowers of rhetoric

Being able to write and speak persuasively is a powerful tool. It can rouse nations into war. Win hopeful leaders elections. It can win hearts, change minds and turn the course of history. It can even get you into hot water. Take a minute to remember the Roman statesman Cicero, whose ability to persuade and deliver powerful speeches was well known across the land. According to historical records, in 43BCE, Cicero was captured and executed by soldiers loyal to Mark Antony. According to ancient sources, his head and hands were severed and sent to Rome as proof of his death. In a ghoulish twist of events, Antony's wife, Fulvia, took the severed head and repeatedly stabbed a hairpin through Cicero's tongue to symbolise the hatred she felt towards this once silver-tongued orator. The persuasive tips that Romans, such as Cicero, and the Ancient Greeks developed are still used today. Every year, I tell my class that this persuasive speech is the literary area they are most practised in, as they have spent their whole lives pleading with their parents to stay up later or not eat their broccoli.

● **Three – that's the magic number**

Patterns of three in writing are where the writer uses single words three times, a phrase three times, a sentence three times. They can even use the sentence's rhythm or syntax in a pattern of three. These patterns of three can be found in classical rhetoric, and while there is no single originator of the concept, we can see its effect everywhere we look. One of the key tenets for a pattern of three is that in a long speech, stopping and using a rule of three will make the message stand out from the crowd and become memorable. It can also cut through the rest of your message to give a quick sound bite that is easily digested. Think of the Trump 2016 presidential campaign where the messages 'Lock her up' and 'Drain the swamp' were used to devastating effect to bring down Hillary Clinton. Patterns of three can also be rhythmically pleasing, making the message more impactful for the reader or listener. For example, 'Snap, crackle, pop' (Rice Krispies advert). Delivering the message in a pattern of three is also an excellent way to encapsulate your main argument or to summarise it for your audience so that those main points are hammered home.

Let's explore some classically structured patterns of three sentences.

▶ Tricolon

Tricolons are built using three parallel parts (words, phrases or clauses). To ensure maximum impact, they should follow a similar pattern and be of a similar length, such as Julius Caesar's famous tricolon: 'Veni, vidi, vici' (I came, I saw, I conquered).

SINGLE WORD + SINGLE WORD + SINGLE WORD + WHAT?

Elegance, allure, sophistication – experience it with our perfume.

PHRASE + PHRASE + PHRASE

To achieve your goals, to improve your health, and to find happiness, you must prioritise self-care.

CLAUSE + CLAUSE + CLAUSE

Support a stronger voice, embrace meaningful change, and create a brighter future by voting for me in the school election.

WHEN? + WHEN? + WHEN?

When students express individuality, when families save money, and when schools embrace diversity, banning uniforms benefits everyone.

Sentence Models for Non-fiction Writing

'EVERY' + 'EVERY' + 'EVERY'

Every animal deserves freedom, every habitat should remain undisturbed, and every species needs natural environments, making it clear that banning zoos is the right choice.

'WITH' + 'WITH' + 'WITH'

With hope in our hearts, with a steely resolve, with a deadeye determination, we must fight on.

▶ Adjective overload

A lot of persuasive travel writing uses a triple-adjective structure to add layers of persuasion to the topic.

ADJECTIVE + ADJECTIVE + ADJECTIVE + WHAT?

This exquisite, tasty, delightful dish is the restaurant's signature dish.

Sultry, sandy, sensual. The Sahara Desert is a must-see attraction in North Africa.

Mountainous. Majestic. Magical. Japan.

or

Mountainous, majestic, magical – Japan.

Japan – mountainous, majestic, magical.

▶ A quick note on bicolons and tetracolons

I started by explaining patterns of three as they are so common in persuasive writing. Still, you can also balance out your persuasive ideas using a bicolon, a pattern of two, or a tetracolon, a pattern of four.

▶ Anaphora

Anaphora, an Aristotle favourite, again uses the idea of a triple repetition of a word or phrase at the beginning of successive clauses or sentences. They don't strictly have to be written in patterns of three, but using more than three can grate on your reader or listener.

WORD + WORD + WORD

To ensure we stay **safe**, to keep our children **safe**, and to make the world a **safer** place, we must ban social media.

PHRASE + PHRASE + PHRASE

We must ban social media **for its** invasion of privacy, **for its** promotion of misinformation, and **for its** detrimental impact on mental health.

▶ Alliteration

Alliteration involves repeating the same consonant sound at the beginning of three or more closely connected words, creating a rhythmic effect. By using alliteration as a persuasive device we can make our reader or listener focus on our words and ensure that our key message is more memorable.

3 × ALLITERATION

Discover the dazzling dynamics, the soothing serenades and the captivating cadences – immerse yourself in music.

▶ Epizeuxis

Epizeuxis uses the immediate repetition of a word or phrase for emphasis or emotional impact. It's like hammering a word into the reader's or listener's mind.

WHAT? + 3 × WORD

Feeling stressed and need to unwind? The answer is reading, reading, reading!

3 × WORD + WHAT?

Reading, reading, reading is the answer to all your problems.

▶ Congeries

A congeries is a rhetorical device that piles word upon word, image upon image, to create an effect. The word 'congeries' means a disorderly collection or jumble and can be used to bombard your reader.

WHAT? (REPEATED) + WHERE? OR WHO?

Relax on pristine sands, savour fresh seafood, soak up the sun, explore tide pools teeming with life, wander through quaint shops brimming with treasures, kayak through crystal-clear waters – create memories that last a lifetime!

A worn leather jacket, tinted goggles, khaki trousers, short hair and a determined gaze – Amelia Earhart was a sight to behold in her aeroplane.

▶ Elaborative diacope

This technique is a deliberate repetition of words separated in a sentence where the intervening words between the repetitions further explain or describe the repeated word or phrase. It's like using the pause to provide more detail.

WHAT? + MORE DESCRIPTION + WHAT?

Take a leap, a life-changing leap – join the army.

WHO? + MORE DESCRIPTION + WHO?

Alan Turing was a genius. A bonafide mathematical genius.

▶ Anadiplosis – the Yoda sentence

Anadiplosis is a rhetorical device that uses a sentence's last word or phrase to start the next. For example, in George Lucas's *The Phantom Menace*, the diminutive green guru Yoda instructs, 'Fear is the path to the dark side. Fear leads to anger. Anger leads to hate. Hate leads to suffering'.

WHAT? + YODA (ANADIPLOSIS)

Our cause fights for justice. Justice demands action. Action starts with you. Join us!

▶ Using metaphors to persuade

A well-placed metaphor can persuade your reader by making the main point memorable, by drawing attention to it or by getting them to think about it differently.

WHAT? + METAPHOR

Learning a new skill is like planting a seed. With a little care and attention, it will blossom into something valuable and rewarding.

METAPHOR – WHAT?

A precious jewel in the Mediterranean Sea – Cyprus has something for everyone.

▶ Using the sound of the sentence

We can use the sound of a sentence to capture our reader's attention and create our desired effect. This can be done by using words with similar prefixes or suffixes. Or we can use the words' consonance (consonant sounds), assonance (vowel sounds) or cadence (the timing or the flow of a sentence).

3 × SUFFIX 'ING'

Whether exercising, studying or just relaxing at home, music is so important in many people's lives.

ASSONANCE

Witness their willpower, their skills soaring, and support the superstars of women's football.

CONSONANCE

Fast footwork, and fierce finesse, fuel the future of football – watch the women's game take flight.

▶ Using personification

Giving human qualities to non-living things, ideas or even abstract concepts makes them more relatable and easier to understand. Personification can tap into your reader's feelings and can strengthen your argument.

NOUN + PERSONIFICATION

The oceans, once teeming with life, are now choked by plastic waste.

The forests, the lungs of the Earth, are gasping for breath under the relentless assault of deforestation.

Sentence Models for Non-fiction Writing

▶ Hyperbole

Hyperbole, or as my colleague once embarrassingly referred to it as the American football-sounding Hyper-Bowl, is an excellent technique to persuade your audience. Using it sparingly can grab your reader's attention and make the message more memorable.

NOUN + HYPERBOLE

Our gym will have you feeling like a superhero in weeks!

(Of course, you don't expect to develop X-ray vision and be able to fly, but it shows that you will make a big improvement.)

VERB + HYPERBOLE

Every penny you donate to our charity will make a world of difference.

(Of course, a penny won't save the world, but it helps give importance to your contribution.)

● Talking to your reader – direct address

EXPLAIN

Direct address: We ___ but ___ .

We all take for granted ___ but ___ .

2 × 'WE'

We need to do more to help. We need to take action now.

2 × VERB

Stand up for your rights. Stand up for your fellow citizens.

2 × ADVERB

The undeniably efficient electric car is undeniably the future of transportation.

2 × ABSTRACT NOUN

To truly understand the importance of world peace, one must understand that it is the foundation upon which all human progress and happiness depend.

STATE THE OPPOSITE

Stop wasting your time. Start making a difference.

3 × ADJECTIVES

Bold, brave and brilliant – Marie Curie was the first woman to win the Nobel Peace Prize.

Marie Curie, bold, brave and brilliant.

3 × RHETORICAL QUESTIONS (DIRECT ADDRESS)

Do you want to leave a lasting impression wherever you go? Are you ready to indulge in a luxurious experience? Wouldn't you love to have a scent that's as unique as you are? Luxe, the new scent from Maison Du Parfum.

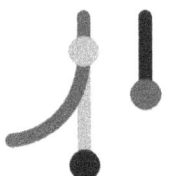

Chapter 12
Why the writing isn't working and what to do about it

Many years ago, I decided I wanted a peep behind the wizard's curtain and signed up for the KS2 Writing Moderator Training. Travelling around my local area, visiting schools and reading hundreds of students' writing was the best writing CPD I've ever had, and it has crystallised in my mind why writing doesn't work.

First, let me give you some context. To become a moderator, you have to sit a standardisation exercise. These are normally made up of three collections of work, each from a different student, containing five or six pieces of writing. In preparation for this, local authorities deliver all the associated training by following a script, from which I am told they are not allowed to deviate. The sessions I have attended have always been well explained and the people in charge are knowledgeable and, in my opinion, do a fantastic job.

In the training, you sit with fellow potential moderators, normally Year 6 teachers, and analyse exemplar materials. I am always impressed with the high level of discussion you get and how knowledgeable everyone is about writing. As a group, you look at various pieces of writing and everyone agrees (mostly) what standard they are.

However, I've sat in these exercises and seen people with years of experience have heated rows about whether the lack of a semicolon would stop a child from reaching the greater depth standard (GDS). A fellow teacher reported on Twitter (X?) that, one year, at least 70% of the moderators they sat the test with had failed. Many years ago, I witnessed a room turned, one by one, by an experienced moderator, who I think may have been channelling the film *12 Angry Men*, to each downgrade their judgement from GDS to EXS (expected standard). *Note – the experienced moderator got it wrong and a few teachers who had years of moderating experience refused to sit the test again.*

These exercises are hard. I know, I failed my first two and, in my first year of trying, missed out on being a moderator. Sitting the test, you can twist yourself in knots, second-guessing what the Standards and Testing Agency (STA) is looking for and what the person opposite you looks like they're writing on their sheet. People commonly say they are going to 'go with their gut'. I understand this and have said it myself. But is this what we want our students' writing to be judged by? A teacher's gut feelings?

The reason I mention my moderation experiences here is that if you ask anyone, they will state that subjectivity is the main problem with assessing writing. I often see online a piece of student writing held up as GDS that is overwritten. I have worked with many teachers who have underestimated the writers' quality in their class. One poor stressed Year 6 teacher told me she'd have to fail her whole class as they didn't know about complicated things such as coordination. She was relieved when I told her that a compound sentence using 'and' would do the job.

Taking part in these moderation exercises helped me understand the assessment issues that every educator faces when assessing writing. Assessment is not just a problem for year groups whose writing needs to be moderated externally. Across the world, there are teachers who every day have to grade a piece of writing or decide what assessment strands they can highlight. If anything, the teachers with access to moderation at least get another pair of eyes on the writing. It becomes harder and harder to assess in year groups where it is just down to your school, your team, or just you, if working in a small school with a single form entry.

So why the division? Why do we have moderators failing the test each year? Why do we have teachers getting their judgements so wildly wrong? I think one answer comes from our definition of consistency. Let's go back to the KS2 moderation to illustrate this. A good example of consistency is mentioned in the Year 6 assessment framework statement: 'Use verb tenses consistently and correctly'. This is the keyword if you read the Department for Education commentaries for collections that don't meet the expected standard. In each one, spelling, sentence structure, formality and the clarity of meaning are all highlighted as inconsistent. Now, if you have read all the commentaries for every collection (something I have done but wouldn't recommend), you will start to see this pattern emerge. Have all moderators or teachers read every commentary or the collections we look at during the training? What about the Year 6 teachers who are making the initial judgements? In fact, for the first few years, many of these new collections and their commentaries were kept away under lock and key, and we were instructed not to take any copies with us from moderator training sessions. This always seemed daft to me. Why hide it from the people that need it the most? They are available online, but do all teachers know they are there? There is a link in the bibliography to KS2 moderator materials (Lancashire County Council, no date).

To look at this problem more closely, let's look at the collection of writing from pupil B in 2022.

I've worked my way through the five pieces and highlighted an extract below from the KS2 Teacher Assessment Framework (Standards and Testing Agency, 2018) considering them against what can be found in the collection.

- write effectively for a range of purposes and audiences, selecting language that shows good awareness of the reader (e.g. the use of the first person in a diary; direct address in instructions and persuasive writing)
- in narratives, describe settings, characters and atmosphere
- integrate dialogue in narratives to convey character and advance the action
- select vocabulary and grammatical structures that reflect what the writing requires, doing this mostly appropriately (e.g. using contracted forms in dialogues in narrative; using passive verbs to affect how information is presented; using modal verbs to suggest degrees of possibility)

Chapter 12 Why the writing isn't working and what to do about it

- use a range of devices to build cohesion (e.g. conjunctions, adverbials of time and place, pronouns, synonyms) within and across paragraphs
- use verb tenses consistently and correctly throughout their writing
- use the range of punctuation taught at Key Stage 2 mostly correctly (e.g. inverted commas and other punctuation to indicate direct speech)
- spell correctly most words from the Year 5 / Year 6 spelling list, and use a dictionary to check the spelling of uncommon or more ambitious vocabulary
- maintain legibility in joined handwriting when writing at speed.

Source: Standards and Testing Agency. Contains material developed by the Standards and Testing Agency for 2018 national curriculum assessments and licenced under Open Government Licence v3.0. https://www.nationalarchives.gov.uk/doc/open-government-licence/version/3/.

By working through the pieces of writing given, you can tick off most of these statements.

Note – I've not highlighted the spelling statement. This statement and the associated Year 5/6 spelling lists (one of the most regressive documents ever to be introduced) have held back good vocabulary teaching since their introduction. I will leave it unhighlighted for now, but let's imagine this statement can be ignored because it is an area of significant weakness. Or, as I have seen people incorrectly do, find in the collection one or two words from the Year 5/6 lists that are spelled correctly and then highlight them.

Ostensibly, pupil B has passed as an expected Year 6 writer. They have everything ticked off and, therefore, can be passed. On top of this, looking at the Working Towards the Standard (WTS) collection from 2017 (pupil Dani), this writing is stronger, and therefore, you might conclude it fits in the EXS bracket.

63

I will add here (subjectively!) that I enjoyed many aspects of this student's writing, and the 'Holes' piece was atmospheric and well written. But, and this is a big but. And I like big butts, and I cannot lie (sorry, I couldn't resist). I made a quick tot-up of the errors in the collection and found the following mistakes:

- verb tense: 7
- missing words: 3
- lack of cohesion in a sentence (it made no sense!): 10
- spellings: 51
- fragments: 5
- run-ons: 4
- punctuation errors: 38.

Does this number of errors seem consistent for a Year 6 writer to be passed up to secondary school as secure in the standard? What do you think? Is there a quantifiable number for this? Or is it all about how it reads? This is something that drives me potty when people are talking about GDS and they say that it just has 'something about it'. It isn't magic or indefinable as to why it reads so well. It's due to cohesion, clarity of ideas and style.

Cohesion is vital in writing. The basic function of writing is to communicate ideas or to convey information. Whether that be in an instruction manual for your new toaster, like 'Don't use it in the bath', or Virginia Woolf's streams of consciousness. When writing loses its cohesion through fragmented sentences, incomplete thoughts, imprecise word choices and punctuation, it loses its ability to communicate.

I feel the 'consistent' part needs more clarification from the STA. We currently work with a system whereby we tick off what students can do and do not keep track of what they can't.

So, what's the answer? Do we start counting the errors? Do we define consistency with rubrics and percentages to hit? I don't think that is the answer. However, I think the word 'consistent' needs more thought. Should we be recording the functional errors as we moderate to gauge cohesion and consistency? Many of our assessment systems track what students can do, but have no areas to track what they can't do.

Chapter 12 Why the writing isn't working and what to do about it

Another problem is that often the negative aspects highlighted in the commentary are so specific to the piece you are reading they become unhelpful as a rule of thumb to be used against other pieces of work. Being told that the 'byline (of a newspaper report) is not expressed fully to style' or that a reference to Romeo and Juliet's wedding as 'the wedding of the century' is not fitting of the style for a 14th-century Veronese formal letter (I'm paraphrasing this one, but the gist is there) is not useful when reading a piece about plastic pollution or Henry VIII.

If we are looking for writing that engages, reads cohesively, and expresses itself clearly and emotively, then this number of errors across a collection will always make that difficult. If we were given more guidance on what needs to be consistent across the collections, the process would be easier and lead to more agreement on the judgements.

Another problem we face is the drive to constantly be producing more writing. Days after finishing a persuasive monologue with our class, we can find ourselves launching into writing a gothic horror story. With no time to pause and address the key areas of inconsistency in our students' writing, these errors will continue and be compounded until they latch onto our young writers like barnacles. How often have you started the year and discovered you have writers in your Year 6 or Year 10 classes who still write with tense errors, fragmented sentences and run-ons?

Let's look at another example, writing outcome E from pupil B's collection, and at some of those issues they have with their writing.

- incorrect contractions:

I't

- incorrect tense use:

I raced out the garage like nothing happen.

- fragment:

Sunday afternoon, Doctor Death AKA Doctor Dan came and gave my little sister.

65

Sentence Models for Non-fiction Writing

- lack of control (cohesion):

Sunday afternoon, Doctor Death AKA Doctor Dan came and gave my little sister. On the over hand, I saw an oppertunity to go back into the garage.

- run-on:

Curious, adventurous, and excited I staired deeper into the dark rusty nailse were holding up wooden planks spider webs were dancing in the wind.

- complete loss of control:

I was at the back of the garage and I shone my torch onto this one particular spot are millions of woodlise scattered. When I pushed passed all the heavy boxes When I saw blur bottles on what seamed to be some kind of ruge when I blinked one more time my heart dropped.

The lack of cohesion and consistency makes the writing hard to follow. The accompanying commentary states this: 'There is some effective writing in this collection to meet different purposes and audiences, but weaknesses are evident, and the writing lacks consistency overall.'

In conclusion, we will continue to see judgements as subjective until we have more training around what constitutes cohesion and consistency in writing expected of our students.

So, what can we do about it? First, I would drive to ensure that the basics of writing are fluent and automatic in all your students. Your students need a good grasp of sentence structure, tense use, grammar and punctuation; otherwise, their writing lacks cohesion and is hard to comprehend. We must stop pushing our youngest of students to write full compositions. Instead we need to work with them on ensuring that they can write basic sentences first. Much like place value or number sense in maths, these are the building blocks that will lead to later success.

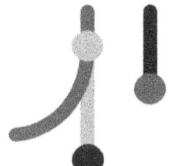 

Chapter 13
Model texts –
putting it all together

I've presented here three model texts (informative, persuasive and biography) that demonstrate how to combine the sentence models in chapters 8 and 11. I have included a quick context and a teacher's guide to the sentence models and writing techniques used for each example.

● An information text

Context: this is a model text I have used to teach students how to write an information text that includes some explanation and is about how earthquakes happen. For this writing, we worked together to create this text on earthquakes, and then the students researched and independently wrote a piece on how volcanoes are formed and erupt.

▶ Earthquakes

An earthquake is an intense shaking of the Earth's surface caused by movements in the Earth's crust.

Earthquakes are created as a result of a fault in the Earth. When the tectonic plates push past each other, pressure builds up along the fault until, eventually, the plates slip, and an earthquake occurs. The energy is released in the form of seismic waves that travel through the rock, causing the Earth to shake. But what happens when an earthquake strikes?

Sentence Models for Non-fiction Writing

Earthquakes can cause widespread devastation and have a profound impact on communities. The most immediate effects of an earthquake include: ground shaking, buildings collapsing, cracks in roads, landslides and damage to infrastructure. Some earthquakes may trigger tsunamis, which can cause massive flooding and destruction along coastal areas. In addition to the physical damage, earthquakes can have long-lasting social and economic consequences, including displacement of populations, disruption of essential services, and damage to infrastructure that can hinder recovery efforts.

▶ Unbelievable facts

- Around 500,000 detectable earthquakes happen annually.
- In Japan alone, there are at least 1500 earthquakes every year.
- Approximately 100 earthquakes a year are big enough to cause damage to properties.

▶ Text features in this writing

An earthquake is an intense shaking of the Earth's surface caused by movements in the Earth's crust.

This is a simple statement (WHAT? + 'IS') sentence to summarise the topic we will write about. It helps clarify for the reader what the information will be about.

Earthquakes are created as a result of a fault in the Earth. When the tectonic plates push past each other, pressure builds up along the fault until, eventually, the plates slip, and an earthquake occurs. The energy is released in the form of seismic waves that travel through the rock, causing the Earth to shake.

This second paragraph explains the opening statement in more detail. The ideas are linked through cause and effect ('when', 'until', etc.). The chronology of earthquakes is followed logically, and precise verbs and vocabulary are used ('created', 'push', 'tectonic plates', 'seismic waves', etc.).

But what happens when an earthquake strikes?

Chapter 13 Model texts – putting it all together

This rhetorical question creates a cohesive paragraph link to the next section.

> Earthquakes can cause widespread devastation and have a profound impact on communities.

The opening sentence summarises the contents of the upcoming paragraph. Again, this is a cohesive link, as the reader knows the upcoming information.

> The most immediate effects of an earthquake include: ground shaking, buildings collapsing, cracks in roads, landslides and damage to infrastructure.

There is a colon for a list sentence that presents the effects.

> Some earthquakes may trigger tsunamis, which can cause massive flooding and destruction along coastal areas. In addition to the physical damage, earthquakes can have long-lasting social and economic consequences, including displacement of populations, disruption of essential services, and damage to infrastructure that can hinder recovery efforts.

I am using 'some' to quantify that not all earthquakes cause tsunamis and to explain the effects of an earthquake in more detail, as well as a pattern of three sentences to list three more effects.

Unbelievable facts

- Around 500,000 detectable earthquakes happen annually.

This section includes bullet points to add further detail and interesting facts. I explain to my students that this is a good place to include information that didn't fit into your main paragraphs but that you think would interest your reader.

● A persuasive letter

Context: this is a model text I have used to teach students how to write a persuasive letter. For this piece, we invited all our students to apply to get a place on our crew for a mission to Mars. Once we had finished our letters, the students were invited to read them to the hiring panel (their teachers), and the best letters won.

> Dear NASA team,
>
> Are you looking for a planet pioneer? Do you need a space crusader? Are you seeking a galaxy gatherer? Then look no further as you have found your new Mission Commander.
>
> Mars has many potential perils. The Red Planet has freezing temperatures of −220 degrees Celsius in the winter, dangerous radiation levels and the hazardous task of landing the craft on a planet covered in deep craters and boulders the size of cars. However, I believe I have the necessary skills to succeed in this mission.
>
> The Mission Commander is an extremely important role in any expedition, as their job is to oversee the whole operation. Being in charge means that you have to be a clear communicator, be calm in stressful situations and make life-or-death decisions. In my simulation training, I demonstrated these key skills when I gave clear instructions to my crew on making a successful landing and made a quick choice on where to safely land our vehicle. But what else would I bring to the role?
>
> In addition to the expertise I showed in the simulated mission, I am a good listener who would take on board the ideas of my crew. Once on the planet, my mastery of maths and science skills would mean that I would quickly be able to lead the building of our shelters and set up our life-support systems.
>
> If I were lucky enough to be chosen, I would bring determination, courage and perseverance to this role. I look forward to hearing from you soon.
>
> Regards,
>
> Mr Youles

Chapter 13 Model texts – putting it all together

▶ Text features in this writing

Are you looking for a planet pioneer? Do you need a space crusader? Are you seeking a galaxy gatherer? Then look no further as you have found your new Mission Commander.

This contains three rhetorical questions to grab your reader's attention, followed by a command to persuade.

Mars has many potential perils.

This is a short sentence for impact with an alliterative pair ('potential perils') to make it memorable for the reader.

The Red Planet has freezing temperatures of –220 degrees Celsius in the winter, dangerous levels of radiation and the hazardous task of landing the craft on a planet covered in deep craters and boulders the size of cars.

Here there is variation of the subject of the sentence ('Mars'/'The Red Planet') to avoid repetition, then a rule of three to show the dangers.

However, I believe I have the skills necessary to succeed in this mission.

This sentence starts with 'however' to show a shift in text from the dangers to myself as the writer to persuade my reader that I should get the job.

The Mission Commander is an extremely important role in any expedition, as their job is to oversee the whole operation. Being in charge means that you have to be a clear communicator, be calm in stressful situations and make life-or-death decisions. In my simulation training, I demonstrated these key skills when I gave clear instructions to my crew on making a successful landing and made a quick choice on where to safely land our vehicle. But what else would I bring to the role?

This section makes a statement and then gives examples for the reader and finishes with a cohesive paragraph link.

If I were lucky enough to be chosen, I would bring determination, courage and perseverance to this role. I look forward to hearing from you soon.

This conditional sentence ('If...') to finish the letter addresses my readers directly and persuades them to hire me.

Sentence Models for Non-fiction Writing

● A biography

Context: we used the fantastic documentary *In the Shadow of the Moon* (2007) to learn about the moon landings. Together, we wrote a biography about Buzz Aldrin, and the students independently researched and wrote a biography about Neil Armstrong. We also read Margot Lee Shetterly's fantastic book *Hidden Figures* (2016).

▶ Buzz Aldrin - a life spent reaching for the stars!

▶ 20 July 1969

Nervously, Buzz held onto the ladder. Hands shaking. Palms sweaty. His mind raced. Gripping the rungs, he cautiously descended. Looking down at the Earth's inviting blue oceans, he wondered if they would make it home. Part one of the mission had been completed, but the greater challenge was yet to come. With a final deep breath, he jumped down from the ladder, but just before his feet touched the ground, time seemed to stop, and his whole life flashed before his eyes...

In the summer of 1969, Buzz Aldrin stepped out onto the Moon and became one of the most famous people in the world. This is the story of his remarkable life.

Buzz Aldrin began life on 20 January 1930, in Montclair, New Jersey. When he was just two years old, his father, who was a colonel in the US Air Force, took him on his first flight, and this gave him an interest in all things air bound.

Because of his love of flying, he joined the Military Academy and when, in 1950, the Korean War broke out, he became a fighter pilot. During his time in the military, Aldrin flew 66 death-defying combat missions. In one particular moment of note, Aldrin courageously shot down two MiGs and was decorated with the Distinguished Flying Cross for his service.

In 1963, Aldrin was part of a group of men selected by NASA to attempt to pioneer space flight. On 20 July 1969, Buzz, along with Flight Commander Neil Armstrong, made the historic Apollo 11 moonwalk, becoming the first two humans to set foot on another celestial body. They spent a total of 21 hours on the Moon's surface: the walk was watched by over 600 million people on television; they collected rock samples from the Moon's

Chapter 13 Model texts – putting it all together

surface and planted the American flag. Upon their safe return to Earth, Buzz was decorated with the Presidential Medal of Freedom; his life in space exploration was now drawing to a close.

After 21 years of service, Aldrin retired. Now in his 80s, Aldrin gives lectures and makes numerous television appearances, including competing on *Dancing with the Stars*, showing the world that the senior astronaut still has some impressive moves. Aldrin has led a life more varied and colourful than most and who knows what life will hold next for this modern-day explorer of the final frontier space.

▶ Text features in this writing

Nervously, Buzz held onto the ladder. Hands shaking. Palms sweaty. His mind raced. Gripping the rungs, he cautiously descended. Looking down at the Earth's inviting blue oceans, he wondered if they would make it home. Part one of the mission had been completed, but the greater challenge was yet to come.

This part focuses on an exciting moment in Buzz Aldrin's life and, by using some storytelling techniques like the senses, short sentences for effect, and capturing his thoughts and feelings it brings the landing on the Moon alive as we experience it from his point of view.

With a final deep breath, he jumped down from the ladder, but just before his feet touched the ground, time seemed to stop, and his whole life flashed before his eyes…

This transition sentence links into the section about his childhood.

Buzz Aldrin, began life on 20 January 1930, in Montclair, New Jersey. When he was just two years old his father, who was a colonel in the US Air Force, took him on his first flight and this gave him an interest in all things air bound.

The time adverbial is here to orient my reader (note – they don't always need to be fronted!). Then comes a link into the next section using a statement ('all things air bound' links to the next paragraph as it is about Buzz becoming a pilot).

Because of his love of flying, he joined the Military Academy and when, in 1950, the Korean War broke out, he became a fighter pilot.

73

Sentence Models for Non-fiction Writing

> *During his time in the military, Aldrin flew 66 death-defying combat missions. In one particular moment of note, Aldrin courageously shot down two MiGs and was decorated with the Distinguished Flying Cross for his service.*

This paragraph starts with a fronted subordination sentence to explain why he became a pilot. The rest of this section shows how to use the correct time adverbials to create cohesion within the retelling of your subject's life.

> *In 1963, Aldrin was part of a group of men selected by NASA to attempt to pioneer space flight. On 20 July 1969, Buzz, along with Flight Commander Neil Armstrong, made the historic Apollo 11 moonwalk, becoming the first two humans to set foot on another celestial body. They spent a total of 21 hours on the Moon's surface: the walk was watched by over 600 million people on television; they collected rock samples from the Moon's surface and planted the American flag. Upon their safe return to Earth, Buzz was decorated with the Presidential Medal of Freedom; his life in space exploration was now drawing to a close.*

This section can be used to teach how cohesion can be created through the control of your tenses. This can be especially tricky for a student when writing a biography. The last sentence uses a semicolon to show how the two clauses are linked.

> *After 21 years of service, Aldrin retired. Now in his 80s, Aldrin gives lectures and makes numerous television appearances, including competing on* Dancing with the Stars, *showing the world that the senior astronaut still has some impressive moves. Aldrin has led a life more varied and colourful than most and who knows what life will hold next for this modern-day explorer of the final frontier space.*

The final section uses time adverbials for cohesion, but also varies this by using a sentence starting with the subject ('Aldrin...'). It ends with the author's voice as they explain to the reader what the future might or might not hold.

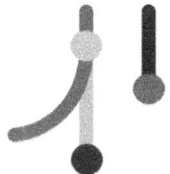 

Appendices

Useful phrases

▶ Biography

▶ Early life
- Born and raised in ___
- From a young age, (he/she/they) displayed a talent for ___
- The formative years spent in ___ were crucial in shaping ___

▶ Milestones and achievements
- A turning point came in ___ when ___
- This experience proved to be a catalyst for ___
- (His/Her/Their) dedication paid off when ___
- This breakthrough led to ___

▶ Challenges and overcoming obstacles
- Despite facing ___ (he/she/they) persevered through ___
- This setback only fuelled (his/her/their) determination to ___
- Overcoming the adversity of ___ , (he/she/they) emerged stronger ___

▶ Impact and legacy
- (His/Her/Their) work has had a lasting impact on ___
- This legacy continues to inspire ___
- Even today, (he/she/they) is/are remembered for ___

Sentence Models for Non-fiction Writing

▶ **Transition phrases**
- In the meantime ___
- Conversely ___
- As a result ___
- Subsequently ___
- Following this success

▶ **Information text**

▶ **Introducing a Topic**
- In this report, we will explore...
- This essay will examine...
- To begin, it is important to understand...

▶ **Presenting Information**
- According to...
- Research suggests that...
- It is widely believed that...
- For example...
- Furthermore...
- In addition to...
- Moreover...
- Consequently...
- As a result...
- This leads to...

▶ **Cause and Effect**
- Due to...
- As a consequence of...
- This is caused by...
- The effect of this is...

Appendices

▶ **Comparing and Contrasting:**
- Similarly...
- Likewise...
- In contrast...
- However...
- On the other hand...
- Despite...

▶ **Concluding:**
- In conclusion...
- To summarize...
- Therefore...
- In summary...
- Based on the evidence presented...

▶ **Adding Emphasis:**
- It is crucial to note that...
- Significantly...
- Importantly...

▶ **Connecting Ideas:**
- Building on this idea...
- Relating to this point...
- To further illustrate...

▶ **Discussion Text**

▶ **Introducing the Topic & Stating Opinions**
- In my opinion...
- I believe that...
- From my perspective...
- It seems to me that...
- I would argue that...

- I contend that...
- I strongly support/oppose...
- This issue raises important questions about...
- Let's consider the following points...

▶ **Presenting Arguments**
- Firstly, it is important to note that...
- Secondly, we must consider...
- Furthermore...
- Moreover...
- In addition to this...
- One of the key arguments is...
- Another important point to consider is...
- This is supported by the evidence that...
- Research suggests that...

▶ **Counterarguments**
- However, it is also important to acknowledge...
- On the other hand...
- Some may argue that...
- It is true that...
- While it is true that..., it is also important to consider...
- Despite this argument...

▶ **Reaching a Conclusion**
- In conclusion...
- To summarize...
- Based on these points...
- Therefore, it is clear that...
- I believe the most compelling argument is...
- Ultimately, the evidence suggests that...
- In my view, the most effective solution is...

▶ Persuasive text

▶ Introducing the Argument
- It is essential that...
- We must recognise the importance of...
- There is a compelling need for...
- I strongly advocate for...
- It is imperative that we...
- To ensure a better future, we must...

▶ Presenting Arguments
- Firstly, it is crucial to consider...
- Secondly, it is evident that...
- Moreover, it is undeniable that...
- Furthermore, research has shown that...
- This is supported by evidence that...
- For instance...
- To illustrate this point...

▶ Emphasising Points
- Undeniably, ...
- Without a doubt, ...
- It is imperative that we...
- This is of paramount importance because...
- We cannot ignore the fact that...
- It is crucial to remember that...

▶ Addressing Counterarguments
- While some may argue that..., it is important to remember that...
- Although it is true that..., the evidence suggests...
- Despite these concerns...
- It is acknowledged that...

Concluding
- In conclusion, it is clear that...
- Therefore, it is imperative that we...
- Based on the evidence presented, it is evident that...
- I strongly urge that...
- Ultimately, the most effective course of action is...

Call to Action
- We must take action to...
- It is our responsibility to...
- I urge you to consider...
- Let us work together to...

Analytical writing

Introducing the Topic
- This essay will analyse...
- The purpose of this analysis is to...
- This analysis will examine...
- This essay will explore the underlying themes of...
- To understand [topic], it is crucial to examine...

Presenting Analysis
- A key feature of... is...
- The author uses... to...
- This can be interpreted as...
- This suggests that...
- The use of [literary device] serves to...
- This technique effectively conveys...
- The author's intention in using... is to...

▶ **Interpreting Meaning**
- This symbolises...
- This represents...
- This can be seen as a metaphor for...
- The author may be suggesting that...
- This reflects the author's...
- This highlights the importance of...

▶ **Comparing and Contrasting**
- In contrast to...
- Similarly to...
- While [one aspect] is..., [another aspect] is...
- The author contrasts... with... to...
- This differs from... in that...

▶ **Drawing Conclusions**
- Ultimately, the work suggests that...
- In conclusion, it can be argued that...
- This analysis reveals that...
- The overall effect of [technique] is to...
- This work provides a powerful commentary on...

▶ **Supporting Your Analysis**
- For example...
- For instance...
- This is evident in...
- As seen in...
- This is supported by...

Bibliography

Camerer, C., Loewenstein, G. and Weber, M. (1989) 'The curse of knowledge in economic settings: an experimental analysis', *Journal of Political Economy*, 97(5), pp. 1232–1254.

Lancashire County Council (no date) *Key Stage 2 Moderator Materials*. Available at www.lancashire.gov.uk/lpds/teaching-and-learning/primary/assessment/moderator-materials/key-stage-2-moderator-materials/ (Accessed 13 November 2024).

Standards & Testing Agency (2018) *Teacher assessment frameworks at the end of key stage 2*. Available at www.gov.uk/government/publications/teacher-assessment-frameworks-at-the-end-of-key-stage-2 (Accessed 13 November 2024).

Tidd, M. (2016) *The Four Purposes of Writing*. Available at https://michaelt1979.wordpress.com/2016/08/29/writing-for-a-purpose-or-4/ (Accessed 13 November 2024).

Zinsser, W. (1976) *On Writing Well: The Classic Guide to Writing Nonfiction*. New York: HarperCollins Publishers.